HOW DO WE KNOW ABOUT POMPEII?

The Roman writer Pliny the Younger was an eyewitness to the eruption of Vesuvius in AD 79. He described it in great detail in a letter to the historian Tacitus. His uncle, Pliny the Elder, was commander of the Roman fleet at Misenum (see map, page 5), and died while trying to rescue his friends by sea. Volcanic eruptions of this kind are now called "Plinian eruptions."

The ash that covered Pompeii preserved many of the buildings, even down to the furniture and wall decorations. This makes it one of the most important and exciting archaeological sites in the world. The nearby town of Herculaneum was buried by mud. So far, only parts of it have been excavated.

Author:
John Malam studied ancient history and archaeology at the University of Birmingham, England, after which he worked as an archaeologist at the Ironbridge Gorge Museum in Shropshire. He is now an author, specializing in nonfiction books for children. He lives in Cheshire with his wife and their two young children. Find out more at: www.johnmalam.co.uk

Artist:
David Antram was born in Brighton, England, in 1958. He studied at Eastbourne College of Art and then worked in advertising for fifteen years before becoming a full-time artist. He has illustrated many children's nonfiction books.

Series creator:
David Salariya was born in Dundee, Scotland. He has illustrated a wide range of books and has created and designed many new series for publishers in the UK and overseas. In 1989 he established The Salariya Book Company. He lives in Brighton with his wife, illustrator Shirley Willis, and their son Jonathan.

Editor: **Stephen Haynes**

Editorial Assistant: **Mark Williams**

© The Salariya Book Company Ltd MMVIII
No part of this publication may be reproduced in whole or in part, or stored in a retrieval system, or transmitted in any form or by any means, electronic, mechanical, photocopying, recording, or otherwise, without written permission of the publisher. For information regarding permission, write to Scholastic Inc., 557 Broadway, New York, NY 10012.

Published in Great Britain in 2008 by
The Salariya Book Company Ltd
25 Marlborough Place, Brighton BN1 1UB

ISBN-13: 978-0-531-18748-7 (lib. bdg.)   978-0-531-16900-1 (pbk.)
ISBN-10: 0-531-18748-9 (lib. bdg.)   0-531-16900-6 (pbk.)

All rights reserved.
Published in 2008 in the United States
by Franklin Watts
An imprint of Scholastic Inc.
Published simultaneously in Canada.

A CIP catalog record for this book is available from the Library of Congress.

Printed and bound in China.
Printed on paper from sustainable sources.

You Wouldn't Want to Live in Pompeii!

Written by
John Malam

Illustrated by
David Antram

Created and designed by
David Salariya

A Volcanic Eruption You'd Rather Avoid

Franklin Watts
An Imprint of Scholastic Inc.
NEW YORK • TORONTO • LONDON • AUCKLAND • SYDNEY
MEXICO CITY • NEW DELHI • HONG KONG
DANBURY, CONNECTICUT

Contents

Introduction

The year is AD 79, and you are in Pompeii, a small, pleasant Roman town in the south of Italy. You've spent most of your life here, but Pompeii isn't your hometown. You were born in Greece, and Greek is your first language, although Latin is the language of the Roman Empire. As a young man you were taught to read and write in Greek, and you learned about the poets, writers, and thinkers of Greece. You had dreams of becoming one of them yourself.

But you were captured by pirates, who sold you to a slave dealer. You became the property of a wealthy Roman family. You've been with them so long, you're one of the family now, but don't get any ideas—you're still a slave! Now, as an older man, you've become a *paedagogus*—a slave who looks after your master's son at home and at school. You're his buddy, whether he likes it or not.

The long, hot summer of AD 79 starts like all those that have gone before it—but soon you will wish you were anywhere but in Pompeii!

Greetings, friends!

POMPEII'S PLACE. Pompeii is in the region of Campania. It's one of many towns along the coast, and is the nearest to Mount Vesuvius, the region's highest hill.

Earthquake! Flashback to AD 62

Damage Across the Region

HERCULANEUM. This nearby town suffered major damage to its public buildings, and people were very frightened.

NAPLES. Less damage was caused here, as the town was farther from the center of the quake.

ANIMALS. A flock of 600 sheep dropped dead of shock near Pompeii.

STATUES. As the ground shook, statues wobbled until they cracked and fell.

A good slave works hard, doesn't complain, and doesn't run away. Most of all, a slave should be loyal, obedient, and trustworthy. You proved how useful you were when you saved your owners' lives. It was 17 years ago, when an earthquake rocked Pompeii and the surrounding countryside. As buildings fell, you led your master and mistress to safety. You put their lives before your own, and almost died when a roof tile hit your head. That tremor was a warning sign from Vesuvius. The hill was slowly waking from its long sleep—but no one realized this at the time.

What is it?

February 5, AD 62

Look, a sign!

EMPEROR SURVIVES EARTHQUAKE.
In AD 64 there was another earthquake. Emperor Nero was in Naples, acting in a play. He was unharmed, and took this as a sign that the gods were protecting him.

SLEEPING GIANT. Close to Pompeii is Mount Vesuvius. Some say that it poured forth monstrous fire in ancient times, but it doesn't now.

Handy Hint

Protect your master and mistress. Then they will be kind to you—they will not get rid of you.

Master! Mistress! This way! Come on!

Fix It! Rebuilding Pompeii

The earthquake of AD 62 is now a distant memory. Today, in AD 79, life has returned to normal for the people of Pompeii. Most of the buildings damaged in the earthquake were repaired long ago, but in a few places builders are still at work even now.

Over the years, your owners have been good to you. When their son was born, they made you his paedagogus—his own personal slave. It's an important and responsible job. An educated Greek like you makes the best companion for the son of a wealthy Roman. You must teach him your wisdom and knowledge.

EARTHQUAKE PICTURE. This carving in stone shows buildings damaged in the quake of AD 62.

MOSAIC PICTURE. *Tesserae* —tiny cubes of colored stone— are used to make long-lasting mosaic floors.

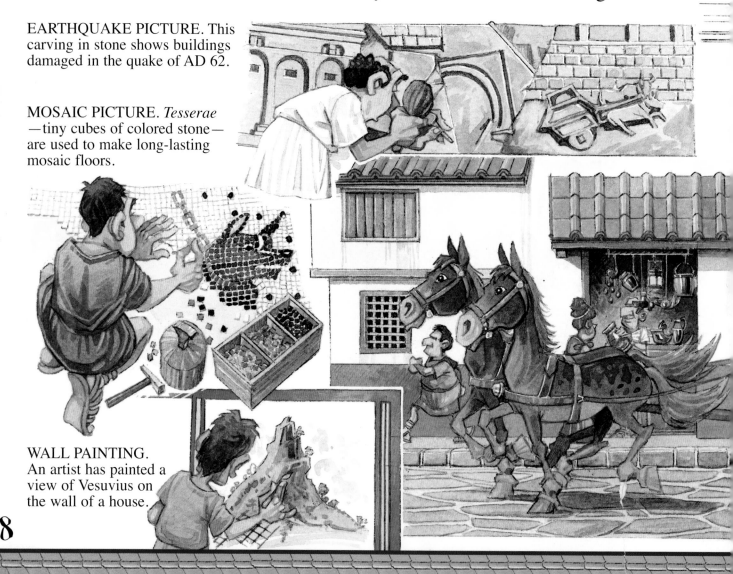

WALL PAINTING. An artist has painted a view of Vesuvius on the wall of a house.

August 20, AD 79

The boy loves to hear the story of how you saved his parents from the earthquake—and each time you tell it, it gets better! Like the Greek storytellers of old, you go on and on, weaving an ever grander tale. You're even starting to believe it yourself!

A hundred tiles fell on my head!

Liar!

No way!

Old scoundrel!

Cool!

School! Looking after Your Master's Son

It's expensive to send him to school. Make sure it's money well spent.

Clap!

Pay attention to the teacher!

Long ago, the famous Greek philosopher Plato said, "A sheep can no more live without a shepherd than a boy without a paedagogus." And so it is—you are like a shepherd for your master's son. Without you to take him to school, and watch over him in class, he would be like a little lost lamb. You are his companion and friend. You are always there for him. At school, a *magister* (teacher) will teach him reading, writing, and possibly numbers, but you will give him his real education. You must prepare him for adult life, instructing him about the ways of the world, and how a good Roman should behave in public and in private. Tell him what is right and wrong, and what is good and bad. Do these things well, and your master can ask no more of you.

GET UP. Wake him at daybreak. Open the window to let light into his bedroom.

GET WASHED. Bring him a bowl of water so he can wash his face and hands.

GET DRESSED. Help him take off his nightshirt, then put on his tunic and sandals.

Either learn or leave!

I can see smoke!

GET TIDY. Hand him a comb and make sure he uses it! His hair should be neat and tidy.

GET PACKED. You carry his inkstand, pens, books, and writing tablets in a *scrinium*.

GET GOING. Then set off for the schoolroom. As a slave, you must walk behind the boy.

11

Day Out! A Visit to a Vineyard

Your owner is a businessman. He plans to buy a large quantity of grapes from vineyards on the slopes of Mount Vesuvius, and turn them into red wine. He'll sell it in the markets of Pompeii, and make a lot of money. Vines grow well in the mountain's fertile soil, but this year the farmers are worried. They're saying that many vines are wilting and starting to die. Instead of swelling with juice, the grapes are shriveling up and will be no good for wine. This news has troubled your owner, so he's gone to a vineyard to investigate, and he's taken you with him. The farmer doesn't know what's killing the vines—and he's even more puzzled by strange wisps of steam and smoke coming from the ground. They smell of rotten eggs!

Around Pompeii

THE RIVER. The Sarno links Pompeii to the sea, and waters the fields.

SEA SALT. At the coast, sea water is evaporated in shallow pools (salt pans) to leave salt crystals.

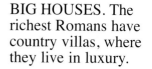

BIG HOUSES. The richest Romans have country villas, where they live in luxury.

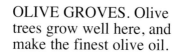

OLIVE GROVES. Olive trees grow well here, and make the finest olive oil.

August 22, AD 79

THE GOD'S OWN MOUNTAIN. Grapes grow so well here that Vesuvius is said to be the home of Bacchus, the god of wine.

GODS' GIFT. The first grapes of the year were picked on August 19, and a lamb was sacrificed to the gods.

Handy Hint

You'll be doing plenty of walking today. Instead of your usual sandals, wear lace-up walking boots.

WHEAT FIELDS. Farmers harvest wheat by hand. The grain makes flour for bread.

SHEEP FARMING. Sheep provide wool and sheepskins for clothing and bedding.

Gladiators! The Games Come to Town

On the east side of Pompeii is the amphitheater—a big open-air building where people watch gladiatorial games and animal fights. It's quite old-fashioned: it has only two entrances, and there's no machinery to move scenery around. Twenty years ago, in AD 59, there was a riot here when visitors from nearby Nuceria came to watch the games. They insulted the Pompeians, spat at them, and tossed seat cushions around. And when someone threw a stone at an official, the Pompeians had had enough. The crowd got onto the sand of the arena and fought like gladiators! Fighting spilled into the streets, and many people were killed. After that, all games were banned at Pompeii for ten years. Enjoy today's show, but keep out of trouble!

Look Out For:

NOTICES. You'll know when the games are coming because painted signs will appear on buildings, with dates and times.

Go for it!

To Vulcan, the best, the greatest!*

Referee

Charon

*The modern word *volcano* comes from the name of the Roman god of fire.

FESTIVAL OF VULCAN. Today, August 23, is the annual festival of Vulcan, god of fire. Watch as priests sacrifice fish and sheep to Vulcan, and ask him to protect Pompeii and its people.

The man dressed as Charon (the ferryman of the underworld) hits the defeated gladiators with his mallet.

August 23, AD 79

GRAFFITI. Fans put names and pictures of their favorite gladiators on walls. It shows who they support.

Handy Hint

Don't upset the Nucerians! They're still annoyed about losing the riot, and they'd love to get even with you!

I'm outta here!

STREET MARKET. Traders set up stalls outside the arena. Buy bread, cheese, pies, fish sauce,** and fruit, which you can eat as you watch the games.

Let him go!

Kill him!

Make my day!

**Very popular! But you wouldn't want to live near the place where they make it.

Little Bang! Vesuvius Wakes Up

The summer of AD 79 has been strangely different from other summers. This year you've noticed many odd things, from dead fish floating in the river to smelly gas escaping from the ground. Are these signs of something bad about to happen? People carry on as usual, but they feel uneasy.

Today begins like any other day. You take your master's son to school, and stay with him as he does his lessons. But when a series of small bangs are heard coming from Mount Vesuvius, you go into the street to see what's happening. Rising from the summit is a dirty grey cloud, and a light rain of ash is falling from the sky. No doubt about it—something very strange is going on!

Warning Signs

TREMORS. The first shakes were felt about four days ago, on August 20. They were quite strong, and cups and plates got broken.

NOISES. With each tremor came a loud booming noise from under the ground.

DROUGHT. Wells and springs that should be full of fresh water have dried up.

FISH. The River Sarno is full of dead fish, as if it has been poisoned.

FUMES. Smoke and gas have started coming out of holes in the ground.

GRAPES. Grapes that should be ripe have withered on the vines.

16

Big Bang! Vesuvius Blows Its Top

People stare in wonder at the cloud rising from Mount Vesuvius. Some begin to panic and run for their lives —but you know that your duty is to stay with your young master. In fading light you make your way through the gloomy streets, taking him home to his parents—no more school for him today!

By midday the air is choked with ash, and day has turned to night. The volcano's gases stink of rotten eggs, and it's getting harder to breathe. You think you will be safe in the house, but you soon realize you were wrong. In the early afternoon, a tremendous explosion rips the top off Vesuvius, and a huge cloud of dust and pumice rises into the sky.

Here's What's Happened

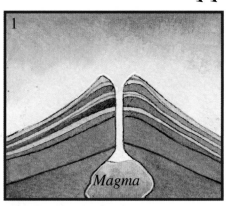

1

Magma

1. MAGMA CHAMBER. A space underneath Mount Vesuvius has filled up with molten rock or *magma*. It's under great pressure.

2. MAGMA RISES. As the pressure increases, the magma is forced out of the chamber and up toward the surface along a *conduit* or pipe.

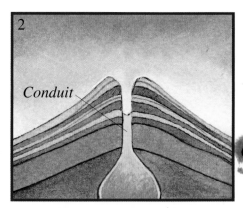

2

Conduit

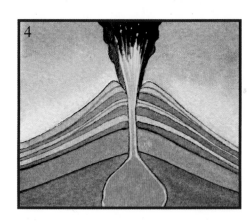

3

Pumice

3. PUMICE. Near the top of the conduit, the red-hot magma cools and mixes with gases to make *pumice*—a lightweight rock filled with air bubbles.

4. EXPLOSION. A high-speed jet of gas rushes along the conduit and forces the pumice and tons of grey ash into the sky. Big bang!

4

August 24, AD 79, 1:00 p.m.

Handy Hint

Say your prayers! Go to the shrine of your household gods and pray that they will spare your life.

It's dreadful!

Wow!

We'll have to go.

12.4 miles

5. ASH CLOUD. Because the gases are lighter than the surrounding air, they rise high into the sky, taking the ash with them.

6. WIND. The wind blows the ash cloud to the southeast, toward Pompeii. Ash falls from the cloud and settles on the town.

Vesuvius

Pompeii

5

6

19

Panic! Pompeii in Chaos

Ash and pumice have been falling steadily for the last five hours. As the layer gets deeper, house roofs sag under the weight, and by late afternoon the first ones collapse. Fear grips the town, and people scramble to get out along the road to Nuceria. They take their money and jewelry with them. Some try to take shelter in your house, but they're not welcome. The sound of pumice clattering onto the building is nonstop, and you have to shout to make yourself heard. Your master packs a chest with his family's most treasured possessions. Soon it will be time for you all to leave.

Help us!

REFUGEES. The people of Pompeii gather up their belongings and leave town.

LOOTERS. Some people seize the chance to steal from the empty houses.

3 ft

8 ft

WHITE TO GREY. As more pumice falls, it changes color from white to grey.

Handy Hint

Keep checking how deep the ash layer is —if it gets too deep you'll be trapped in the house.

Go away!

Keep out!

I'm scared!

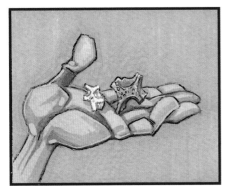

OUCH! Grey pumice is twice the size of the white, and hurts if it hits you.

COLLAPSE. From late afternoon roofs cave in under the weight of the pumice.

BLOCKED. Pumice floats, and it soon clogs up the River Sarno.

Run! It's Time to Leave

Terror on the Streets

It's been the worst day of your life, and it's not about to get any easier. Ash and pumice have been falling onto Pompeii for several hours, and the town is slowly but surely being buried by the fallout from the volcano. Your master has finally decided to leave the house and try to lead his family to safety. But the door won't open, because there's so much ash and pumice stacked against it. You have to climb out through a window. It's soft underfoot, like gritty sand, and the weight of the family's treasure chest pulls you down. With every step you sink to your knees, and walking—or wading—gets harder. Your master and his son protect their heads from falling debris with cushions. The family stays together. They move faster than you, and very soon you are left alone in the choking, noisy darkness.

VOICES. It's now so dark that people cannot see their way. They call out for their loved ones.

Claudia!

Marcus!

Dad!

Mom!

DEAFENING NOISE. The rain of pumice gets stronger. As millions of pieces crash to the ground, it sounds like the roar of thunder.

END OF THE WORLD? People think the world is coming to an end. Some say the gods have deserted them.

LAST GASP. The air is filled with poisonous fumes. People choke as they breathe. Ash and pumice threaten to bury them alive.

It's Over! Well, That's What You Think!

At the very end of this terrible day the hail of pumice slows down, and it's not as noisy as before. People who are still in Pompeii venture into the wrecked streets, and begin to wonder if the nightmare is coming to an end. (It's not. It's really only the quiet before the storm.)

You now feel totally abandoned, with only the family pet for company. As for your owners and their son, you pray to the gods that they found a way to get out of Pompeii, and are now safe from harm. Perhaps one day you will see them again.

As the long, dark hours of night slowly pass, you feel the ground shaking as earthquakes continue to rumble all around. From Vesuvius you hear a booming, roaring noise, as if something very heavy is rolling along the ground. It seems that Mount Vesuvius has not finished with Pompeii yet. What a miserable night!

Danger at Sea

LAST SHIP. Your owners make it to the port, and catch the last ship to leave Pompeii. The harbor is full of pumice floating on the water, and the sea is rough.

GIANT WAVE. Late at night the sea is pulled back from the shore. It comes back as a tsunami and smashes into the coast.

August 24, AD 79, 11:00 p.m.

MORE EARTHQUAKES. All through the night, earthquakes shake the region, and buildings fall to the ground.

Handy Hint

Don't forget the family pet! Tie a cushion to his head to protect him from falling lumps of pumice.

What now?

What now?

The End! Death of a Town

The end comes suddenly. At 6:30 on the morning of August 25, the rest of the cloud of ash and pumice spewed out by Vesuvius begins to fall back to earth. Millions of tons of red-hot volcanic debris surge down the mountainside at great speed, reaching the town wall in minutes.

Those caught by it are suffocated by the deadly fumes. More surges follow, blanketing the streets and buildings.

It is all over in just thirty minutes. Pompeii, the town that 15,000 people had once called home, is buried beneath a deep layer of ash. Only the tops of the tallest buildings can still be seen.

The Last Day of Pompeii

SULPHUR GAS. The choking smell of rotten eggs in the air increases, and it becomes impossible to breathe.

DAYBREAK. The fall of pumice slows down. People make a last attempt to flee from the town.

LIGHTNING. Bolts of lightning flash through the sky, and for a split second they light up what's left of Pompeii.

TOTAL DESTRUCTION. The first surge of boiling ash and pumice reaches the town walls. The next ones overwhelm the town.

August 25, AD 79, 8:00 a.m.

In the days and weeks that follow, survivors dig through the ash to recover statues of the gods. Emperor Titus visits the devastated area the following year. He orders repairs to some towns, but nothing is done for Pompeii. It is left as a graveyard for the 2,000 Pompeians who died in the eruption.

Handy Hint

There are plenty of horses on the loose. Grab one and hold on for dear life as it races to safety.

HEAD FOR NUCERIA. The ash and pumice are not so deep in that direction.

MISSING PERSONS. In Nuceria, you put up notices asking for information about your missing family.

It's the end of everything!

HAPPY FAMILY! Your family hasn't forgotten you. Their ship took them to safety, but they never gave up hope of finding you alive. They saw your notices in Nuceria, and at last you are reunited with them.

Found! Pompeii Uncovered

Dig, Dig, Dig

DIGGING BEGINS. At first, people were only interested in finding statues and valuables.

Pompeii was almost forgotten. Even its true name slipped from memory, and local people referred to it simply as "la cività," meaning "the city." The modern story of Pompeii begins in 1748, when treasure-hunters began the first of many excavations to find valuable objects. In 1763 a carved stone was found that gave the name of the town.

PLASTER CASTS. In the 1860s, Giuseppe Fiorelli poured plaster into hollows in the ash, where bodies had been. It set hard, revealing the body shapes of long-dead Romans.

TOWN PLAN. Most of Pompeii has now been uncovered.

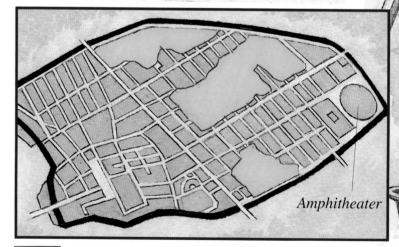

Amphitheater

Areas not yet excavated

Today, Pompeii is a Roman time capsule. As visitors walk along the ancient streets and look into shops and houses, it's as if they have been transported back in time to August AD 79. But just north of the ruins is the sleeping Mount Vesuvius. It's a constant reminder of what destroyed Pompeii—and also preserved it for the future.

Handy Hint

If you're one of the one million people who live near Vesuvius today, watch the volcano closely—and hope it stays asleep!

Lost on August 24, AD 79...

...and found almost 2,000 years later!

ASLEEP AGAIN. Today, Mount Vesuvius is dormant. This means it is not erupting now, but is still capable of erupting. The most recent eruption was in 1944.

29

Glossary

Amphitheater An open-air building where gladiatorial contests and animal hunts were held.

Arena The floor of an amphitheater. *Arena* is Latin for "sand."

Bacchus The Roman god of wine.

Charon In Roman myth, the boatman who ferries souls to the underworld.

Dormant (Referring to a volcano) in a "sleeping" phase, neither **active** (erupting from time to time) nor extinct.

Extinct (Referring to a volcano) having come to the end of its life, so that it will never erupt again.

Gladiator A person who has been trained to fight in the arena to entertain an audience. His main weapon is the **gladius**—a short stabbing sword.

Graffiti Words and pictures scratched or painted onto a wall or other surface.

Looter A person who steals from buildings during an emergency.

Magma Molten (melted) rock under the ground. When it spills onto the surface it is known as **lava**.

Mosaic A picture made from tiny cubes (**tesserae**) of colored stone.

Nero Emperor of Rome, AD 54–68.

Paedagogus (pronounced **pee-da-go-gus** or **pie-da-go-gus**) A slave, often from Greece, who worked for a Roman family. His job was to take his master's son to and from school, and teach him how to be a good Roman citizen. The word means "child guide" in Greek.

Philosopher A thinker or wise person.

Pumice A volcanic rock filled with air bubbles, making it very light in weight.

Refugee A person who has been forced to abandon his or her home.

Riot A wild disturbance by a crowd of people.

Scrinium A container for scrolls and writing implements.

Shrine A miniature temple where prayers can be offered to the gods.

Surge A sudden powerful movement in one direction.

Tablet A wooden board, covered with wax, used for writing on. Letters were scratched in the wax with a point called a **stylus**; the blunt end of the stylus was used to erase letters.

Titus Emperor of Rome, AD 79–81.

Tremor A small earthquake.

Tsunami A huge wave caused by an earthquake or eruption.

Villa A large house in the countryside.

Vineyard A place where grapes are grown.

Vulcan The Roman god of fire.

Index